He has risen.

Matthew 28:6

ZONDERKIDZ

'Twas the Morning of Easter

Requests for information should be addressed to:
Zonderkidz, 3900 *Sparks Dr. SE, Grand Rapids, Michigan* 49546

———————————————

Library of Congress Cataloging-in-Publication Data
Names: Nellist, Glenys, 1959- author.
Title: 'Twas the morning of Easter / by Glenys Nellist.
Description: Grand Rapids, Michigan : Zonderkidz, [2021] | Audience: Ages
   4-8. | Summary: "In the beloved rhythms and rhyme of the classic poem "
   'Twas the Night Before Christmas," 'Twas the Morning of Easter tells the
   story of the resurrection of Jesus in a fresh, inspiring way and
   features joyful illustrations that bring the story to life for
   children"-- Provided by publisher.
Identifiers: LCCN 2020023736 (print) | LCCN 2020023737 (ebook) | ISBN
   9780310769064 (hardcover) | ISBN 9780310769095 (epub)
Subjects: LCSH: Jesus Christ--Resurrection--Juvenile literature. |
   Easter--Juvenile literature. | Bible stories, English.--Gospels.
Classification: LCC BT482 .N45 2021 (print) | LCC BT482 (ebook) | DDC
   232.9/7--dc23
LC record available at https://lccn.loc.gov/2020023736
LC ebook record available at https://lccn.loc.gov/2020023737

———————————————

Zondervan titles may be purchased in bulk for educational, business, fundraising, or sales
promotional use. For information, please email SpecialMarkets@Zondervan.com.

Art direction and design: Cindy Davis

Printed in Malaysia

21 22 23 24 25 IMG 10 9 8 7 6 5 4 3 2

This book is dedicated to one of my wonderful editors, who gave me the idea for it in the first place. Thank you, Barbara, for believing in me. I will forever be grateful.—G.N.

I would like to dedicate this book to my father, the mastermind of all my success.—E.S.

'Twas the Morning OF Easter

Written by Glenys Nellist

Illustrated by Elena Selivanova

ZONDERkidz

'Twas the morning of Easter, before the sun rose,
  Two guards on a hillside were just trying to doze.
You see, Jesus had died, only three days before—
A huge stone had been placed, to seal the cave door.

The disciples were sleeping, but tossed in their beds,
As visions of danger swirled 'round in their heads.
Would *they* be arrested and led away too?
Without Jesus, their leader, what would they do?

In her small, quiet home, not too far away,
Jesus' friend, Mary, was planning the day.
She would go to the cave with perfume and spice,
In hopes that her gifts would make Jesus smell nice.

The sun, through the trees, was just starting to peep
At the guards on the hill who were now fast asleep.
When all of a sudden, there came an earthquake!
And the rocks and the trees all started to shake.

The guards jumped in fright, then fell straight to the floor
As the stone rolled away and unsealed the door.
Then Mary arrived, and crept up to the cave.
She had to see Jesus . . . she had to be brave.

But the cave was now empty! He just wasn't there!
Mary sat down and wept, and her cries filled the air.
But suddenly Mary heard someone behind.
"Dear woman, who is it that you hope to find?"

Mary jumped and turned 'round, so confused and afraid.

Was this man the gardener? And why had he stayed?

But the calm in his voice; the words that he said,

Soon let Mary know she had nothing to dread.

"Dear Mary, it's me! It's Jesus, your friend!
My story's just starting—this wasn't the end!"
His eyes, how they twinkled; his smile so bright—
Mary knew in a moment, but could she be right?

She gasped in surprise and cried, "Jesus! It's you!
You came back to life—your promise came true!"
Jesus nodded and said, "But there's no time to lose—
You must tell the disciples—go! Spread the good news!"

So she jumped to her feet and away Mary went,
She'd a story to tell—a tale heaven-sent!
She ran without stopping, and called through the door,
"Disciples, you've never heard *this* news before!"

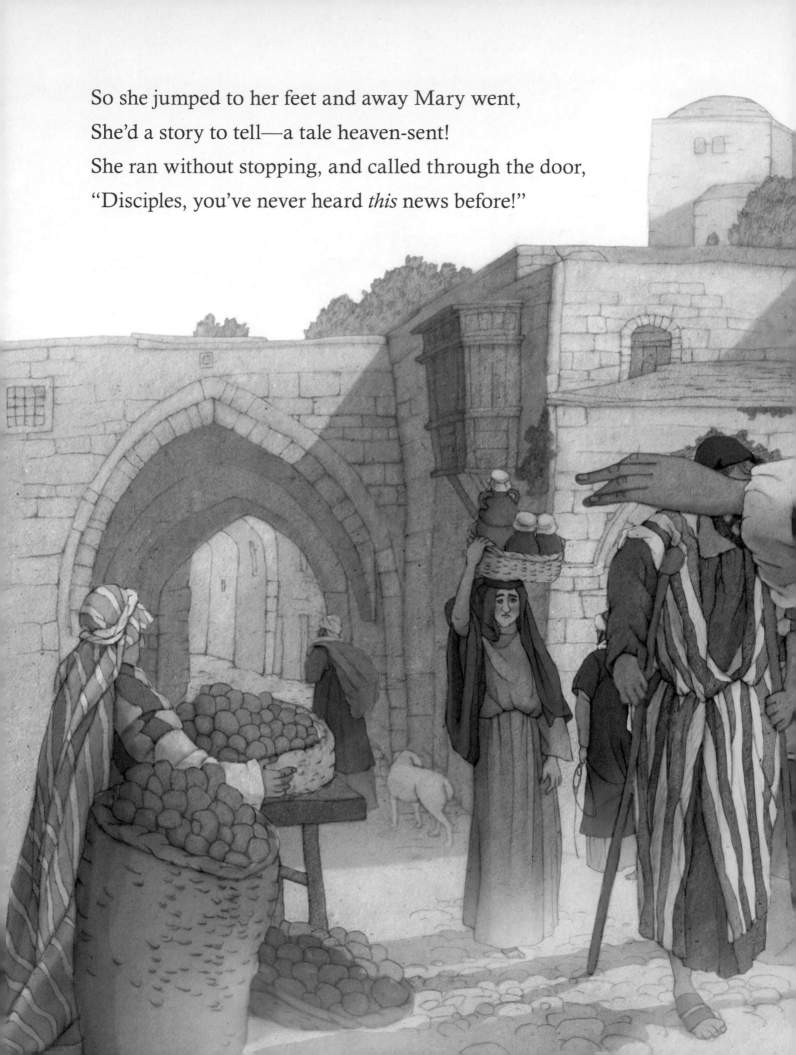

"Now Peter, now James, now Thomas, now John!
I went to the cave—Jesus' body was gone!
But he called me by name—he's alive! It is true!
It's a miracle only our great God could do!"

Then the trees seemed to dance; birds started to sing.

All creation joined in to worship the King.

"He's alive, he's alive!" the rocks cried in praise.

The whole earth rejoiced on this day of all days!

When later that night, Mary knelt down to pray,
She thought about all that had happened that day.
And the stars heard her whisper, through soft evening light . . .

"Happy Easter to all, and to all . . . a good night."